Robot Space Explorers

Contents

Written by Rob Alcraft

Collins

Many robots have been **launched** into space.

2

Adventure in deep space

The Voyager robots were launched nearly half a **century** ago. They are still flying through space now.

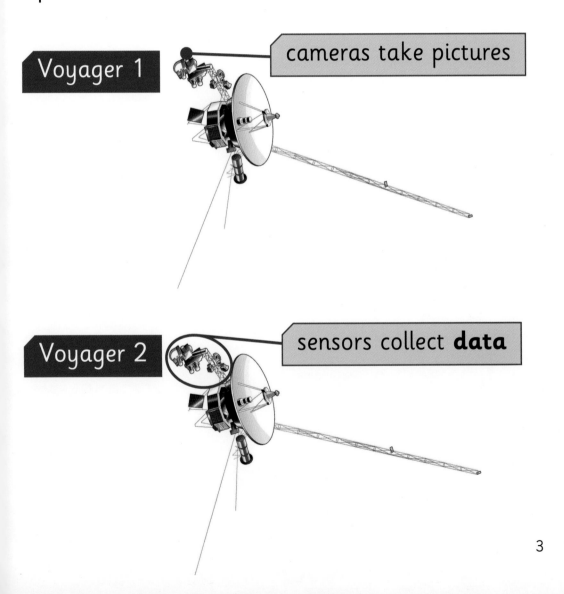

Voyager 1

cameras take pictures

Voyager 2

sensors collect **data**

The Voyagers have taken close-up pictures
of planets.

Jupiter

This patch is
a giant storm.

The Voyagers have sent data back to scientists on Earth. Voyager 1 flew very close to Saturn. It was able to study the planet's rings.

rings of dust and ice

Nothing has ventured further from Earth than the Voyagers.

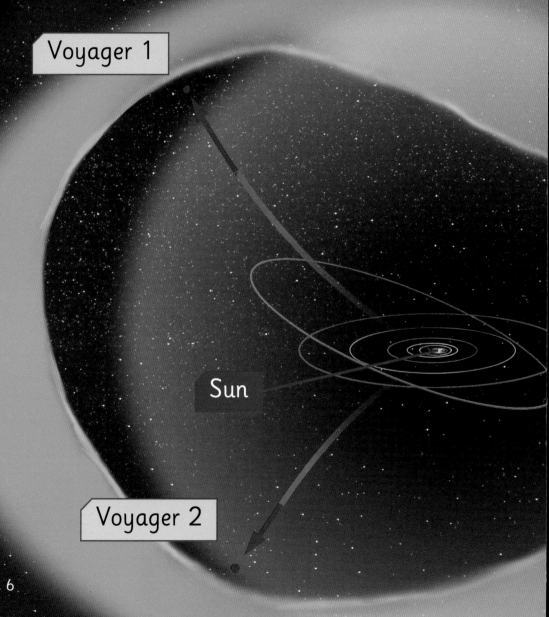

Voyager 1

Sun

Voyager 2

Voyager 1 took this picture of Earth from very far away.

Earth

Scientists need giant listening devices to capture data from the Voyagers.

Comet landing

The Rosetta robot's task was to carry a **probe** into space and land it onto a comet.

solar panels
supply energy

sensors collect
data

Rosetta's probe

Comets are left-over lumps of planet that hurtle through space. Getting close to one would not be easy. Some comets glow brightly and are visible from Earth.

It took over ten years for Rosetta to catch up with the comet.

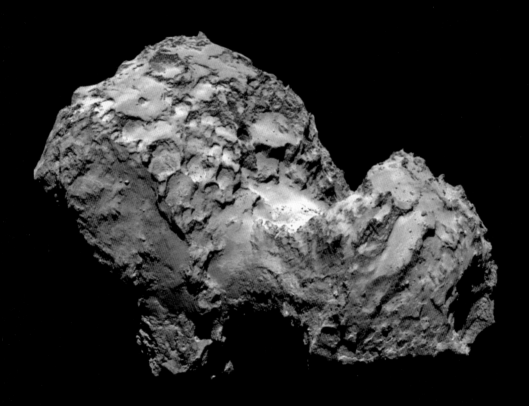

This picture shows the comet named 67P.

Rosetta followed the comet through space. When it was very close, it released its probe down onto the comet.

Rosetta's probe

This blurry picture shows Rosetta's probe, nestled in a shadowy crevice.

Rosetta's probe took pictures and sent data back to scientists on Earth.

Rosetta's work showed that Comet 67P was like a huge dirty snowball. It was a mixture of rock, ice and chemicals.

Rosetta's incredible work was now done. Scientists sent Rosetta on a slow final dive into the comet, collecting data as it went.

A last picture – then Rosetta was wrecked.

Working on Mars

Right now, wheeled robots named rovers are hauling themselves across the dusty plains of Mars.

Rovers on Mars are searching for water and evidence of life.

Landing on Mars is difficult. All a robot's **technology** must work perfectly.

This robot crashed when something went wrong.

parachute

protective wrapping

This is a picture taken by a rover on Mars.
At night, while it snoozes, the robot shares data
with scientists on Earth.

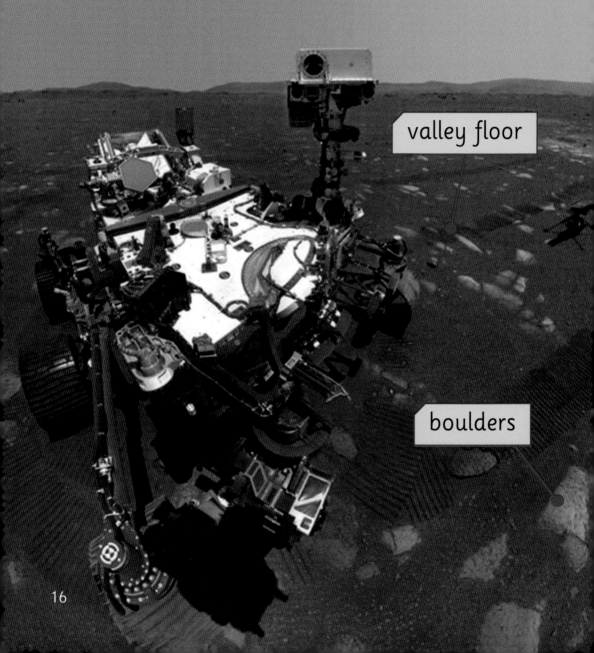

valley floor

boulders

Mars has giant volcanoes and deep **chasms**.
The temperature at night is like a freezer.

volcano

Could humans follow robots to Mars?
Rovers are testing technology that could prepare
for future human visits.

a Mars rover at work

Robots in space

Robots can go where humans can't. They have ventured into other worlds and are showing us the wonders of the universe.

Glossary

century 100 years

chasm a very deep hole or valley

chemicals the basic ingredients of everything

data numbers and facts

launched fired into the air

probe a mini space-craft

technology machines and computers

Index

Robots exploring space

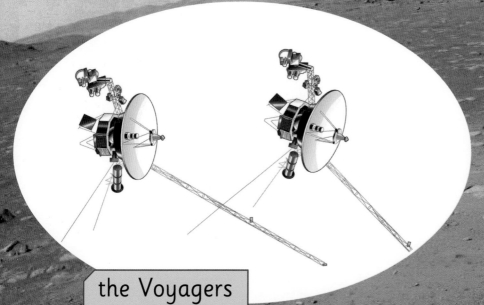

the Voyagers

Rosetta

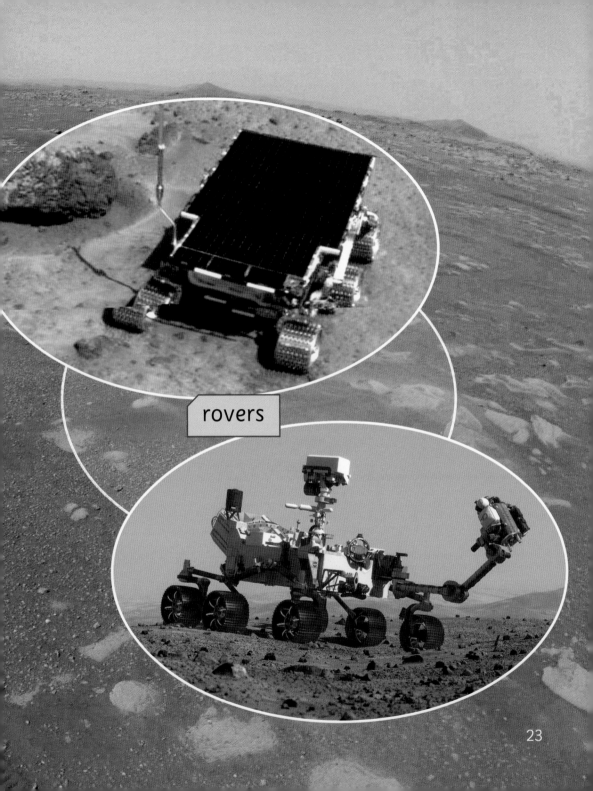

rovers

🐾 Review: After reading 🐾

Use your assessment from hearing the children read to choose any GPCs, words or tricky words that need additional practice.

Read 1: Decoding

- Ask the children to read these words, and identify the letter/s that make the sounds:

  /ch/ **ventured** (*ture*) **patch** (*tch*)   /or/ **hauling** (*au*) **water** (*a*) **floor** (*oor*)

  /s/ **listening** (*st*) **scientists** (*sc*)   /ur/ **Earth** (*ear*) **worlds** (*or*)

- Challenge the children to read a page aloud fluently. Say: Can you blend in your head as you read?

Read 2: Prosody

- Model reading pages 2 and 3 to the children as if you are a television presenter.
  - Challenge the children to pick a page and practise reading it with expression.
  - Ask children to read their page out loud, and encourage positive feedback on tone, pace and emphasis.

Read 3: Comprehension

- Hold a group discussion on robots. Ask the children: What do you know about robots? What did you know about robots before you read this book? What information in the book surprised you most? Why?
- Discuss the title, and ask: Do you think it's a good title for this book? Why? Can you think of a better one?
- Ask the children to talk about the meaning of the following words in the context of each page:
  - page 11 **nestled** (e.g. *lies comfortably*)
  - page 16 **snoozes** (e.g. *stops working for a while*)
- Display the following words without their page numbers. Ask the children to think of words with similar meanings (synonyms) to the following:

  explorers (page 2)   **close-up** (page 4)   **devices** (page 7)   **capture** (page 7)
  - Ask the children to find each word on the page, and read the sentence with their replacement word. Ask: Does the sentence still make sense? If not, why?
- Turn to pages 22 and 23, and ask the children to choose a photo. Ask them to scan the text to find information about the photo before feeding back to the group.